Hal•Leonard
JAZZ PLAY-ALONG®

Book and CD for B♭, E♭, C and Bass Clef Instruments

JOHN COLTRANE
GIANT STEPS

VOLUME 149

Arranged and Produced by Mark Taylor

T0081827

ISBN 978-1-4584-2217-0

Hal•Leonard®
CORPORATION

7777 W. Bluemound Rd. P.O. Box 13819 Milwaukee, WI 53213

Visit Hal Leonard Online at
www.halleonard.com

JOHN COLTRANE GIANT STEPS

Volume 149

Arranged and Produced by
Mark Taylor

Featured Players:

Graham Breedlove–Trumpet
John Desalme–Saxes
Tony Nalker–Piano
Regan Brough–Bass
Jim Roberts–Bass
Steve Fidyk–Drums
Todd Harrison–Drums

Recorded at Bias Studios, Springfield, Virginia
Bob Dawson, Engineer

HOW TO USE THE CD:

Each song has <u>two</u> tracks:

1) Split Track/Melody

Woodwind, Brass, Keyboard, and **Mallet Players** can use this track as a learning tool for melody style and inflection.

Bass Players can learn and perform with this track – remove the recorded bass track by turning down the volume on the LEFT channel.

Keyboard and **Guitar Players** can learn and perform with this track – remove the recorded piano part by turning down the volume on the RIGHT channel.

2) Full Stereo Track

Soloists or **Groups** can learn and perform with this accompaniment track with the RHYTHM SECTION only.

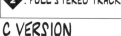

COUNTDOWN

C VERSION

BY JOHN COLTRANE

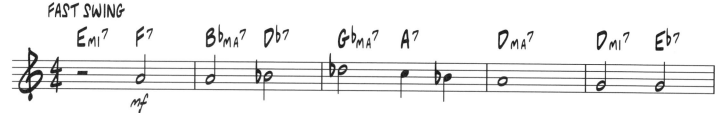

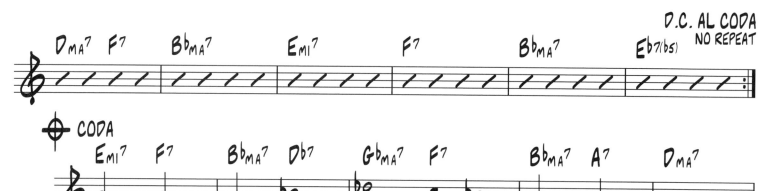

COUSIN MARY

C VERSION

BY JOHN COLTRANE

GIANT STEPS

BY JOHN COLTRANE

MR. P.C.

CD
◆ 7 : SPLIT TRACK/MELODY
◆ 8 : FULL STEREO TRACK

C VERSION

BY JOHN COLTRANE

SPIRAL

BY JOHN COLTRANE

C VERSION

SYEEDA'S SONG FLUTE

CD
⬩13⬩ : SPLIT TRACK/MELODY
⬩14⬩ : FULL STEREO TRACK

BY JOHN COLTRANE

C VERSION

NAIMA
(NIEMA)

BY JOHN COLTRANE

C VERSION

NAIMA
(NIEMA)

BY JOHN COLTRANE

COUNTDOWN

Bb VERSION

BY JOHN COLTRANE

COUSIN MARY

BY JOHN COLTRANE

CD
3 : SPLIT TRACK/MELODY
4 : FULL STEREO TRACK

Bb VERSION

GIANT STEPS

BY JOHN COLTRANE

CD

⑤ : SPLIT TRACK/MELODY
⑥ : FULL STEREO TRACK

Bb VERSION

MR. P.C.

Bb VERSION

BY JOHN COLTRANE

SPIRAL

BY JOHN COLTRANE

CD
- 11 : SPLIT TRACK/MELODY
- 12 : FULL STEREO TRACK

Bb VERSION

SYEEDA'S SONG FLUTE

BY JOHN COLTRANE

Bb VERSION

COUNTDOWN

BY JOHN COLTRANE

Cousin Mary

CD
❸ : SPLIT TRACK/MELODY
❹ : FULL STEREO TRACK

Eb VERSION

BY JOHN COLTRANE

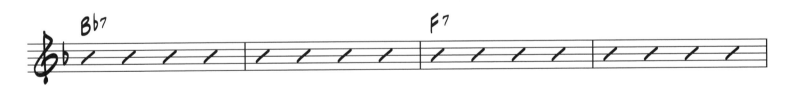

D.C. AL FINE
WITH REPEAT

CD

GIANT STEPS

BY JOHN COLTRANE

Eb VERSION

FAST SWING

TO CODA ⊕

SOLOS (11 CHORUSES)

D.C. AL CODA
WITH REPEAT

⊕ CODA

MR. P.C.

BY JOHN COLTRANE

Eb VERSION

SPIRAL

BY JOHN COLTRANE

CD

13 : SPLIT TRACK/MELODY
14 : FULL STEREO TRACK

SYEEDA'S SONG FLUTE

BY JOHN COLTRANE

Eb VERSION

MEDIUM SWING
PLAY 2ND X ONLY

CD

◆ 9 : SPLIT TRACK/MELODY
◆ 10 : FULL STEREO TRACK

NAIMA
(NIEMA)

BY JOHN COLTRANE

Eb VERSION

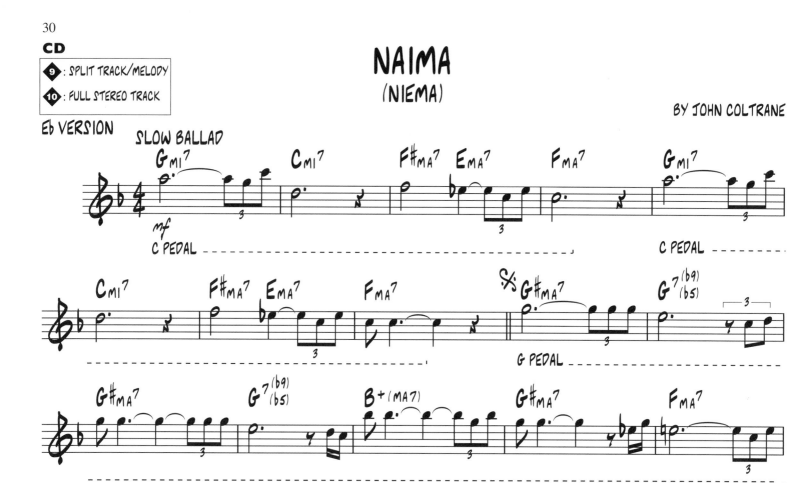

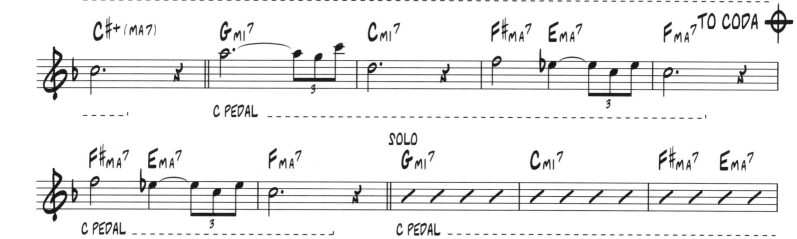

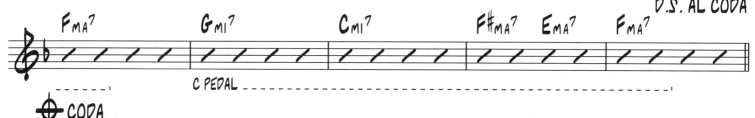

NAIMA
(NIEMA)

BY JOHN COLTRANE

COUNTDOWN

BY JOHN COLTRANE

COUSIN MARY

GIANT STEPS

BY JOHN COLTRANE

CD
5 : SPLIT TRACK/MELODY
6 : FULL STEREO TRACK

𝄢 : C VERSION

MR. P.C.

BY JOHN COLTRANE

SPIRAL

BY JOHN COLTRANE

SYEEDA'S SONG FLUTE

BY JOHN COLTRANE

1A. MAIDEN VOYAGE/ALL BLUES
00843158 ....$15.99

1. DUKE ELLINGTON
00841644.......................$16.95

2. MILES DAVIS
00841645.......................$16.95

3. THE BLUES
00841646.......................$16.99

4. JAZZ BALLADS
00841691.......................$16.99

5. BEST OF BEBOP
00841689.......................$16.95

6. JAZZ CLASSICS WITH EASY CHANGES
00841690.......................$16.99

7. ESSENTIAL JAZZ STANDARDS
00843000.......................$16.99

8. ANTONIO CARLOS JOBIM AND THE ART OF THE BOSSA NOVA
00843001.......................$16.95

9. DIZZY GILLESPIE
00843002.......................$16.99

10. DISNEY CLASSICS
00843003.......................$16.99

11. RODGERS AND HART FAVORITES
00843004.......................$16.99

12. ESSENTIAL JAZZ CLASSICS
00843005.......................$16.99

13. JOHN COLTRANE
00843006.......................$16.95

14. IRVING BERLIN
00843007.......................$15.99

15. RODGERS & HAMMERSTEIN
00843008.......................$15.99

16. COLE PORTER
00843009.......................$15.95

17. COUNT BASIE
00843010.......................$16.95

18. HAROLD ARLEN
00843011.......................$15.95

19. COOL JAZZ
00843012.......................$15.95

20. CHRISTMAS CAROLS
00843080.......................$14.95

21. RODGERS AND HART CLASSICS
00843014.......................$14.95

22. WAYNE SHORTER
00843015.......................$16.95

23. LATIN JAZZ
00843016.......................$16.95

24. EARLY JAZZ STANDARDS
00843017.......................$14.95

25. CHRISTMAS JAZZ
00843018.......................$16.95

26. CHARLIE PARKER
00843019.......................$16.95

27. GREAT JAZZ STANDARDS
00843020.......................$16.99

28. BIG BAND ERA
00843021.......................$15.99

29. LENNON AND MCCARTNEY
00843022.......................$16.95

30. BLUES' BEST
00843023.......................$15.99

31. JAZZ IN THREE
00843024.......................$15.99

32. BEST OF SWING
00843025.......................$15.99

33. SONNY ROLLINS
00843029.......................$15.95

34. ALL TIME STANDARDS
00843030.......................$15.99

35. BLUESY JAZZ
00843031.......................$16.99

36. HORACE SILVER
00843032.......................$16.99

37. BILL EVANS
00843033.......................$16.95

38. YULETIDE JAZZ
00843034.......................$16.95

39. "ALL THE THINGS YOU ARE" & MORE JEROME KERN SONGS
00843035.......................$15.99

40. BOSSA NOVA
00843036.......................$16.99

41. CLASSIC DUKE ELLINGTON
00843037.......................$16.99

42. GERRY MULLIGAN FAVORITES
00843038.......................$16.99

43. GERRY MULLIGAN CLASSICS
00843039.......................$16.99

44. OLIVER NELSON
00843040.......................$16.95

45. GEORGE GERSHWIN
00103643.......................$24.99

46. BROADWAY JAZZ STANDARDS
00843042.......................$15.99

47. CLASSIC JAZZ BALLADS
00843043.......................$15.99

48. BEBOP CLASSICS
00843044.......................$16.99

49. MILES DAVIS STANDARDS
00843045.......................$16.95

50. GREAT JAZZ CLASSICS
00843046.......................$15.99

51. UP-TEMPO JAZZ
00843047.......................$15.99

52. STEVIE WONDER
00843048.......................$16.99

53. RHYTHM CHANGES
00843049.......................$15.99

54. "MOONLIGHT IN VERMONT" AND OTHER GREAT STANDARDS
00843050.......................$15.99

55. BENNY GOLSON
00843052.......................$15.95

56. "GEORGIA ON MY MIND" & OTHER SONGS BY HOAGY CARMICHAEL
00843056.......................$15.99

57. VINCE GUARALDI
00843057.......................$16.99

58. MORE LENNON AND MCCARTNEY
00843059.......................$16.99

59. SOUL JAZZ
00843060.......................$16.99

60. DEXTER GORDON
00843061.......................$15.95

61. MONGO SANTAMARIA
00843062.......................$15.95

62. JAZZ-ROCK FUSION
00843063.......................$16.99

63. CLASSICAL JAZZ
00843064.......................$14.95

64. TV TUNES
00843065.......................$14.95

65. SMOOTH JAZZ
00843066.......................$16.99